Original title:
Shooting Star Serenades

Copyright © 2025 Creative Arts Management OÜ
All rights reserved.

Author: Vivian Laurent
ISBN HARDBACK: 978-1-80567-788-8
ISBN PAPERBACK: 978-1-80567-909-7

Stardust's Secret Song

In the night sky, a spark did jump,
A comet with a silly bump.
It whistled tunes of funky jive,
Making space critters come alive.

With tails a-swish and grins all wide,
They danced in orbits, side by side.
Galactic laughter filled the scene,
As they twirled like a glittering machine.

Guiding Lights of the Universe

A friendly moon with goofy beams,
Guides lost stars in wild dreams.
"Follow me!" it crooned with glee,
"Let's play hide and seek, just you and me!"

But stars tripped over cosmic dust,
"You're it!" they giggled, filled with trust.
The sun peeked out, with a playful grin,
"Looks like the game is set to begin!"

Harmony Among the Constellations

Orions danced in goofy pride,
While Ursa danced with wobbly side.
Each constellation shared a laugh,
As meteors formed a silly path.

The Big Dipper tried to spin,
But tripped on stars; oh, what a din!
They rolled and tumbled with such delight,
Creating chaos in the night.

Celestial Rhapsody

Jupiter sang with a raspy voice,
While Saturn twirled without a choice.
"Let's make a jam!" they all agreed,
With cosmic banjo, oh, what a deed!

Planets joined in, a merry band,
With meteors clapping, hand in hand.
They rocked the cosmos, bright and bold,
In rhythms of laughter, purest gold.

Fleeting Glimmers

A twinkle flares, it's here, then gone,
I blink, and it's just a con!
Is that a star, or my neighbor's light?
I say, 'Hey, where's my wish tonight?'

With cosmic snacks, we'll laugh and snack,
As meteors zoom in a rambunctious pack.
I tossed a hope, and caught a friend,
Shooting stars are where the laughs ascend!

Grab your pens, and write a wish,
My dog thinks he's the star, delish!
We laugh until we see it fade,
A cosmic joke that fate has played.

Oh twinkling lights, so quick to flee,
Next time, can you stay for tea?
The sky's a hoot, with endless jest,
These fleeting glimmers are the best!

Nightingale's Odyssey

A nightingale hums a quirky tune,
As stars wink like they've had too much moon.
They dance through skies, all bold and bright,
Do they trip on clouds, or take flight?

With a flip and a flap, they twirl around,
Singing silly songs without a sound.
Across the heavens, a jesters' flight,
'Time to sing, and spark the night!'

Their giggles blend with our own delight,
As we chase their laughter, oh what a sight!
With a starlit chorus, we join the show,
As nightingales chuckle, and shimmer the glow.

In a cosmic quest, they serenade,
With quirky stunts that never fade.
To be so free, with laughter so grand,
In the night's bliss, we all take a stand!

Serene Paths of Stardust

In stardust lanes, where silliness reigns,
Each grain giggles, like it's on trains!
With paths ablaze in wobbly glee,
Who knew the cosmos liked to be free?

Frolicking through these twinkling streets,
Comets strut, shaking their beats.
With every bounce a chuckle sprouts,
In our dazzling adventure, we sing out loud!

"Oh look, a star!" we point and cheer,
But they just wink, "You think we're here?"
As shadows dance in cosmic height,
The universe giggles into the night.

But hey, we dance on this stellar stage,
Where silly laughter is all the rage.
So skip along these paths above,
In the stardust glow, our spirits shove!

Wishes on the Winds of Twilight

As twilight whispers, a secret delight,
I wish on whims, like a kite in flight.
With chuckles tossed on the evening breeze,
I ponder if wishes laugh with ease.

"Oh starry friend, do you take requests?"
But it just sways in celestial vests.
A ripple of giggles, such a vast spread,
As I dream of cake—maybe a bread!

As whimsical breezes tickle my nose,
I'll toss out a wish that everybody knows.
"Make me the jester of this great show!"
And the winds reply, "Well, here we go!"

So, here's to wishes, ridiculous and bright,
Let laughter echo through the night.
In twilight's charm, take a wild ride,
With wishes aloft and laughter as our guide!

Nightfall Whispers

The moon's a big cheese wheel, so bright,
It rolls through the sky, what a sight!
The stars gather round for a dance,
In pajamas, they twirl, they prance.

A comet zips by, wearing a hat,
Makes the night giggle, how about that?
The constellations play hide and seek,
With winks and nudges, they're feeling cheeky.

Venus is blushing, oh what a tease,
While Mars is just munching on cosmic cheese.
The Milky Way sparkles, a spread of delight,
While aliens chuckle, all through the night.

So next time you gaze at the sky up high,
Remember the fun that's going by.
The universe grins with a twinkling cheer,
As nightfall whispers their secrets near.

Celestial Echoes

In the vast cosmic sea, there's a fish,
It swims with a moonbeam to grant every wish.
Saturn's rings sparkle like tinsel and gold,
A party in space, if only we're bold.

Jupiter's spinning like it's got ants,
Urging the stars to join in its dance.
The asteroids chuckle, they're rolling in glee,
While meteor showers just want to pee.

A sunbeam's a boogie, always in style,
It shines like a spotlight with a cheeky smile.
The planets take turns, it's a rock 'n' roll band,
In the arena of night, they make their stand.

So let's join the laughter, let's burst into song,
For echoes of night are where we belong.
With cosmic giggles, we dance and we sway,
In the rhythm of starlight that brightens our way.

Stardust Dreams

In a dream where stardust spins like a whirl,
The stars have a secret, as they giggle and twirl.
Asteroids be bouncey balls in the game,
While rockets wear pajamas, feeling no shame.

A black hole burps, what a thunderous sound,
It swallows the light in a spacey round.
Cosmic kittens chasing comets so fast,
Leave trails of laughter, it's a blast!

Nebulae's colors are here to delight,
Like candy floss clouds all fluffing the night.
The solar system's having its fun,
With meteor tea parties, oh what a run!

So close your eyes and let's float away,
To stardust dreams where we laugh and play.
The universe beckons with a tickle and cheer,
In this whimsical realm, we have nothing to fear.

Luminous Trails

With a wink from the sun, the day takes a bow,
While the stars sneak out for a nightly pow-wow.
Galaxies giggle, with twinkles so sly,
They whisper funny jokes as they zoom on by.

Orion's in tights, looking fit, oh dear,
While the Bear is just dancing, full of good cheer.
Pluto throws glitter, it's a marvelous sight,
As galaxies glide in a shimmery flight.

Uranus plays pranks with its cheeky spin,
It's the king of the night, with a mischievous grin.
Cassiopeia boasts of her glamorous flair,
While comets all blush, caught up in the air.

So as you look up at the vast velvet night,
Remember the laughter that twinkles in sight.
For every bright star holds its own secret tale,
In the infinite sky with illuminated trails.

Aurora's Caress

Bright lights dance in the night sky,
They tickle the clouds as they fly.
A comet wears a clownish nose,
And giggles as it playfully glows.

Whispers of laughter fill the air,
As meteors launch without a care.
They need a friend for their delight,
To join the fun in the soft moonlight.

Planets spin with a silly grin,
Dancing 'round as if in a spin.
They toss confetti made of stars,
Cheering on the joke among Mars.

A rainbow trails through a dark veil,
A cosmic story, a farcical tale.
With every flicker, they play and tease,
Creating chuckles on cosmic breeze.

Nova's Embrace

In a flash, the bright ball explodes,
Like a party popper on heavy loads.
With sparkles flying a mile wide,
And laughter bubbling like a joyous tide.

Galaxies swirl in goofy loops,
Dancing along with jovial groups.
They break out in a cosmic dance,
As aliens join in at a chance.

A comet tries a breakdance spin,
But trips and lands in a bright chagrin.
Yet laughter echoes, clear and bold,
In this cosmic circus, absurd and gold.

With each new twinkle and each new flare,
Laughter surrounds us; it's everywhere!
Stars keep telling their craziest jokes,
As the universe giggles in tangled strokes.

Twilight's Serenade

The sky blushes in a silly hue,
While crickets chirp a funny tune.
As stars debut with goofy winks,
In the starlit hours, the universe thinks.

Fireflies flicker like tiny lights,
In a cosmic game of hide and flights.
They play tag in a twinkling show,
While the moon laughs at its silvery glow.

Clouds drift by, wearing silly hats,
While comets shine with clownish spats.
Each twinkling star feels like a jest,
Inviting us to their galactic fest.

Gravity pulls some pranks and jives,
As planets spin and giggle alive.
Let's sway to the rhythm of the night,
In Twilight's laughter, everything's bright!

Celestial Rhapsody

Planets hum a ridiculous song,
As they dance in orbits all day long.
They poke at each other, making sly faces,
In this cosmic ballet with silly paces.

Asteroids whirl with chaotic grace,
Playing tag in this vast, open space.
A nebula sings with exuberance,
Creating hues that cause a merriment chance.

Stars play peek-a-boo in the night,
Flashing laughter, turning wrongs to right.
Each constellation connects with glee,
Merging worlds where we all want to be.

A symphony of chuckles, wild and free,
From the edge of the galaxy to our knee.
In the vastness of space, we clap and cheer,
For this celestial rhapsody, loud and clear!

Starlit Invocation

In the night sky, bright dots play,
They wobble and wiggle, like kids at a bay.
Wish upon me, the odd little chap,
I'll grant you a giggle, a sprinkle, a slap!

Bouncing and zooming in skies full of glee,
Chasing my tail like a cat, can't you see?
I'll tickle your dreams, while you snooze with a grin,
But watch out for comets; they'll catch you on chin!

Ephemeral Lights

Glimmering sparkles up high in the black,
They've got plans for mischief; they're ready to snack.
Puppies and kittens have gathered to prance,
While starlight spins tales, come join in the dance!

"Catch me!" they giggle, and scamper around,
Like fireflies dodging a cat on the ground.
With laughter that echoes through realms of delight,
Let's hitch a ride on these giggly sights!

Astral Outpourings

A star takes a tumble, and oh what a sight,
Performing its stunts in the soft moonlight.
With cartwheels and flips, it winks and it spins,
When wishes form puddles and laughter begins!

"Is it raining stars?" asks a voice with a cheer.
"No, it's the fun fair, come closer, my dear!"
With sprinkles of sparkle and whimsical mirth,
Let's mingle with magic, our hearts take their birth!

Dreamweaver's Dance

In the dreamscape, where jests never cease,
Each twinkle and twirl brings raucous release.
I've got a funny hat, and a sparkly shoe,
Let's boing through the cosmos, just me and you!

With a hop and a skip, we dance by the sun,
Stumbling and giggling, oh isn't this fun?
Collecting our laughter, we toss it around,
In this show of the stars, we're forever unbound!

Chorus of Comets

In the sky, they zoom and glide,
Whizzing by with a comical ride.
Juggling dreams in their bright tails,
Spreading laughter, they leave their trails.

One tripped over a moonbeam beam,
With a giggle, it lost its gleam.
They tease the planets, oh so bold,
Their antics more than tales of old.

Celestial Cascade

Falling down like cosmic confetti,
Stars in a dance, oh so petty.
Each twinkle, a wink and a jest,
Giggling softly, they never rest.

One whispered secrets to the night,
Causing meteors to take flight.
With a flick, they light the sky,
Laughing as they zoom on by.

Twilight's Embrace

In twilight's arms, stars bounce and play,
Mischief lurking at the end of the day.
They trade jokes with the fading sun,
A cosmic roast, all in good fun.

One tried to fashion a starry hat,
But it rolled off, imagine that!
They tumble down, bright sprites of glee,
Painting the dusk with their jubilee.

Captured in Light

In a flash, they zip and zoom,
Lighting up the velvet gloom.
Caught in laughter, they wiggle and twirl,
Creating chaos, a stellar whirl.

One stole a glimpse from a distant sun,
Shouting, 'Look at me, I'm number one!'
They tease the asteroids, join the fray,
In the grand ballet of night and day.

Cosmic Melodies

In the night sky, a dance unfolds,
Cats chase comets, brave and bold.
Laughing planets spin a tale,
As moonbeams tickle a cosmic whale.

Galaxies giggle, twinkling bright,
While asteroids play tag, what a sight!
Jupiter juggles, Saturn sings,
And Venus hosts the snarkiest things.

Elusive stardust slips away,
As meteors host a wild buffet.
Celestial chuckles echo high,
With cosmic clowns that dance and fly.

So grab your telescope, take a peek,
Watch the universe do the funky streak!
With every blink, magic appears,
Joy fills the cosmos, wiping out fears.

Glimmering Wishes

Under a sky so deep and vast,
Wishes jump on a comet's blast.
Tickling stars with glowing hands,
Making confetti of dreamy plans.

Whimsical rockets zoom and glide,
Silly astronauts with nothing to hide.
Laughter bubbles in the dark,
As fireflies join the wishing park.

Dancing shadows of playful dreams,
With giggles heard from far-off beams.
Moon's bouncy castle, cloud's slide,
Each wish a ride on a cosmic tide.

So toss your thoughts into the sky,
Join the parade as wishes fly!
With glittering hopes, they intertwine,
Under the laughter of the divine.

Ethereal Flight

Winging through the moonlit haze,
Fairies giggle in starlit bays.
Dancing on rainbows, floating high,
With marshmallow clouds that always sigh.

A cosmic chicken struts its stuff,
While silly elves try to act tough.
In a breeze of giggles, they all sway,
As twinkling lights join in the play.

Whirling around on a comet ride,
Joyous sprites take us all inside.
With candy canes and lollipop skies,
Sprinkling cheer, they laugh and fly.

So come join us in this flight,
Where every moment feels just right.
On wings of whimsy, we'll soar above,
In the embrace of cosmic love.

Constellation Lullabies

Stars weave tales of giggly friends,
As bedtime beckons, laughter transcends.
A sleepy bear hums a tune,
While fireflies jam beneath the moon.

Constellations, a playful bunch,
Share secrets over a midnight lunch.
With silly stories of stars and zest,
Eternal laughter that never rests.

In the twilight, the sky does sway,
With breezy whispers of games they play.
Comets serenade with vibrant glee,
While dreamy clouds sip chamomile tea.

So cuddle close and drift away,
On planets where the giggles stay.
With stardust dreams that gleefully bloom,
In the arms of a bright, cosmic room.

Illuminated Dreams

Oh, look at that flash, did you see it?
It zoomed by with a zany little split!
A wish on a taco, a dance in the rain,
Hope it lands softly, or we'll go insane!

With glittering sneakers, they're racing the sky,
While giggling comets eat pie flying by.
Chasing a rainbow, they trip on a beam,
Who knew the cosmos was one wild dream?

Beyond the Night

A blinkle-lit jig under a crescent moon,
Whirling and twirling, the stars found a tune.
The Big Dipper's laughing, spilling its drink,
While Orion wears sunglasses—don't you think?

Stardust confetti falls soft as a sigh,
And Venus is winking with mischief up high.
A cake made of starlight, what a sweet treat,
Time to party with space in a dance-off so neat!

Journey Through the Stars

Hop on a rocket, oh zoom, what a ride!
With giggly aliens laughing inside.
They brought funny hats and a kazoo or two,
Making melodies only we hear, boo-hoo!

Asteroids chuckle, they roll like a ball,
As Saturn spins donuts, oh let's have a ball!
We twirl and we swirl through this cosmic parade,
With laughter and cheer, we've got it made!

Celestial Whispers

Under the vastness, they whisper and play,
Stars share their gossip in a light-hearted way.
'Did you hear about Mars? He's beaming with glee,
Said he found a moon that looks just like cheese!'

While Neptune grins wide, with a bubblegum pop,
The Milky Way sings with a playful hip-hop.
In the world of the cosmos, tales twist and twine,
Making each night a delightful design!

Chasing Light

In the dark, we chase the glow,
With jelly beans and nachos,
I slip, I slide, my snack takes flight,
Oh dear, it's a snackless night!

We run like kids on sugar highs,
Underneath those twinkling skies,
I trip on laughter, sent up in glee,
Why is this fun only happening to me?

Through fields of dreams, we spin and twirl,
Men in costumes, do-si-do, a whirl,
A dog comes by, dressed as a cat,
How could a canine be so flat?

The night is weird, but joy is true,
When chasing lights, I'm with my crew,
With every glance, a giggle escapes,
Who knew a laugh could shape our fates?

The Dance of Fates

Underneath the swirling moons,
We pirouette in silliest tunes,
With giddy hearts, we bump and sway,
A troupe of clowns in bright ballet.

Fumbling feet create a show,
My shoe flies off, a perfect throw,
It lands on Bob, oh what a sight,
He grins and twirls, all in delight!

The stars all giggle, I swear it's true,
As we spin round, in crazy view,
Someone's snack bag bursts with cheer,
Popcorn rains down, what a frontier!

The dance goes on, with pratfalls and fun,
In this crazy world, we're never done,
As fate will have it, let's laugh and play,
Who needs a plan on a starry day?

Reflections of the Night Sky

In puddles shimmer, blinks of light,
I jump and splash, oh what a sight,
My friends all giggle at my splash,
But look! There's a frog with a mustache!

The moon winks down, it's quite a tease,
With shining stars that taunt and please,
We try to count them, lose our way,
Was that twelve? No, that's a stray!

With each reflection, laughter blooms,
We dance beneath the twinkling rooms,
The night is wild, our spirits soar,
As gravity takes a playful tour!

Through giggles, swirls, and midnight quests,
We play like children; it's what we do best,
In the reflections of the sky above,
Come share the joy, the laughs, the love!

Constellation's Secret

You've seen the bear, but have you heard?
He juggles stars, it's quite absurd!
With every bounce, he dances too,
Oh look! He's wearing a tutu!

The lone old sailor thinks it's grim,
But even he can't help but grin,
For every star holds a joke inside,
Like tales of fish that learn to glide!

In cosmic whispers, laughter sings,
As every planet shares funny things,
I shout, "A comet's wearing a hat!"
My friends all nod, "We know all that!"

So let us toast to the skies so bright,
To constellations in their funny plight,
With every laugh in the midnight air,
We find the joy that's truly rare!

Embrace of the Skies

In the night, they zoom around,
With flashy trails, no one's profound.
They giggle bright, leave sparks behind,
A cosmic joke, truly unkind.

With popcorn dreams, they race the moon,
Wishing on them, I'll get a boon.
They wink and dance, oh what a sight,
But they never stick, they're always slight.

So grab your snacks and watch the fun,
As they twinkle out, and still, they run.
In laughter, we toast, with cheeks all aglow,
To the silly stars who steal the show!

Ethereal Traces

Whispers of light in the midnight air,
They tumble and roll without a care.
Their giggles echo across the night,
As they race on by, oh, what a sight!

One wobbles back, another does flip,
A cosmic circus, a starry trip.
With each late-night wish, they start to tease,
"Catch us if you can!" on the galactic breeze.

Chasing shadows with a silly grin,
Making bets on who'll lose or win.
While the world sleeps on, they cheer, they play,
A comedy show in the Milky Way!

Starlit Reveries

In the velvet sky, they twirl and prance,
Fools of the night in a giggly dance.
Tickling clouds with a glimmering spark,
They pull off tricks 'til the sky goes dark.

Tick-tock, they wink, and then they freeze,
What's the secret? Just silly cheese!
A rollicking race through the depths of space,
With laughter that echoes from place to place.

My dreams, they chase with a comical flair,
In the quiet, they burst, leaving nothing but air.
When morning comes, we give them a cheer,
For the whimsy they bring, year after year!

Luminous Secrets

Under the cloak of a playful night,
They spill their secrets in bursts of light.
With a wink and a giggle, they dash away,
Leaving us chuckling 'til the break of day.

Whirling through cosmos, they share a joke,
"Wish upon us, or just play a folk!"
Caught in their merriment, we ride the waves,
Among stardust dreams, hilarity saves.

So come on, friends, let's make a plea,
For more of their antics, wild and free!
With laughter as fuel, and wishes as bait,
We celebrate all, under our starlit fate!

Midnight Glimmers

In the sky, a twinkle plays,
Wishing on a bright display.
A moonbeam tickles, laughs in light,
Chasing shadows through the night.

The cat's on guard, a fierce watchdog,
Barks at stars, thinks they're a frog.
With each pop, the blinkers dance,
The cosmos throws a quirky glance.

A comet's tail with glittering flair,
Gives the Milky Way a funny hair.
Joking with the planets, winks abound,
In this cosmic circus, joy is found.

Nighttime giggles, sparkles ignite,
As whirling dreams take playful flight.
The universe chuckles in delight,
Underneath its vast, silly might.

Astral Harmonies

In the vastness, voices sing,
Tune of laughter in everything.
The stars strum sounds soft as a breeze,
While space dust giggles, puts us at ease.

Planets spin in a jig-like dance,
Wobbling moons join in the prance.
Galactic jokes float through the air,
Each one funnier than a sloth's stare.

Meteor showers, a glittering rain,
Hitting Earth, a comical train.
A rock that snoozed and thought it flew,
Woke up laughing, 'What's this view?'

Melodies burst in a vibrant hue,
Cosmic jokes, just for me and you.
In this orchestra of the night,
Every twinkle's a source of delight.

Radiant Reflections

Mirror balls in the midnight sky,
Reflecting giggles as they fly.
Each wiggly star, a wink, a tease,
Playing peek-a-boo with cosmic ease.

Puppies howl at the glowing moon,
Thinking it's just a big balloon.
Shooting through with a happy bark,
Dancing with the shadows in the dark.

Each comet's path leaves tales to share,
Like candles flickering, light as air.
Witty whispers of starlit jest,
In this celestial comedy fest.

Radiance wraps the world in glee,
As echoes of laughter float so free.
With every light, a story's spun,
In the ink of night, we all have fun.

Whispering Comets

Comets whisper as they zoom by,
Painting smiles across the sky.
"Catch me if you can!" they chime,
In this game of cosmic rhyme.

The stars all play hide and seek,
Tickling each other's cheeks.
Galaxies joke in twinkling hues,
Sharing laughter, silly news.

A star sneezes, sprinkles dust,
Creating chaos, it's a must!
Bright sparkles turn into a trail,
And tickle wonders without fail.

So, hoot and holler at the night,
Join the stars in their delight.
Each twinkle's a chuckle, wild and free,
In this universe, come laugh with me!

Ephemeral Lights of Hope

Sometimes they twinkle like a tease,
Wishing for snacks on a cosmic breeze.
They zip and zoom without a care,
Like they forgot their underwear!

If only they knew we're all awake,
Counting their trails, for fun's sake.
They spin and loop, a daring dance,
Not a clue of their fleeting chance.

They wink and giggle, light years apart,
Creating a ruckus, a wild art.
Who needs a wish with such a sight?
With every flash, they spark delight!

So throw your dreams into the air,
Join in their jest, let down your hair.
For in their glimmer, a chuckle's found,
These cosmic wonders, always around.

The Dance of Fading Light

In a galaxy where joy leaps high,
Whirling beams, each one a sly guy.
They stumble, fumble, and make us laugh,
Keeping time, with their dorky gaffe.

With trails of glitter, they make a mess,
No need to worry, no need to stress.
They shimmy and sway, a playful crew,
As if practicing for a cosmic debut.

Bouncing around on celestial floors,
They play hide and seek behind the stars.
When they flop, it's a glorious sight,
Comedic pauses in the night.

So next time you hear that cosmic sound,
Know that laughter is all around.
In the dark, where dreams take flight,
Join in the dance of fading light.

Timeless Echoes in Space

Echoes bouncing through the dark,
A cosmic chorus, hits the mark.
With giggles and snorts that never fade,
Starlight pranks in a celestial parade.

In the shadows where no one peeks,
They tell tales with silly tweaks.
Listen closely, hear them jest,
Space's comedians at their best!

Zipping by with a cheeky grin,
Wishing for donuts, not to thin!
Twinkling laughter fills the void,
With each burst, joy is deployed.

So when you gaze at night's canvas wide,
Remember the fun that they abide.
Let their echoes fill your heart,
In timeless giggles, we all take part.

Crystalline Connections

Out in the dark where the laughter shines,
Twinkling dots break cosmic lines.
They crack jokes in a shimmering code,
Bubbling over on the starry road.

In a realm where time can't hold,
Silly gaffes and stories bold.
Each little spark, a light-hearted wish,
Creating a cosmic, shimmering dish.

With bright bursts, they share a laugh,
Creating a route, a heavenly path.
If you look close, with heart so pure,
You'll find the humor, bright and sure.

So gather around, beneath the sky,
Join in the fun, give it a try!
For in each glimmer, a smile does bloom,
Through crystalline ties, let laughter resume.

Tapestry of Wishes

A wish flew by with a giggle,
It tripped on clouds and did a wiggle.
Landed on a tree, what a sight!
Squirrels joined in, a wild night!

Stars danced around, all aglow,
Cheering for the wobbly show.
A comet winked, 'Is that a joke?'
Even the moon let out a poke.

A rabbit rushed, oh what a scene,
Dressed in dreams, looking so keen.
With every wish, a chuckle shared,
The universe laughed; none were scared.

So if you see a flash up high,
Don't just wish, take a pie!
Throw it gently, give it a whirl,
And wait for the wishes to unfurl!

Nightingale of the Cosmos

A nightingale sang in galactic streams,
With melodies richer than brightest dreams.
It flapped its wings, oh so spry,
While planets laughed, spinning by.

Its voice bounced off the comet's edge,
The Milky Way made a fun pledge.
'We'll dance and sing, come join the spree,
But keep your socks on, or you'll be free!'

Asteroids twirled, in jovial chance,
While meteors joined in an awkward dance.
With each high note, the stardust flew,
A symphony of laughter, bright and true.

So if you hear that cosmic song,
Just wave your arms, and join along.
The universe hums when we're all afoot,
Celebrating wishes in a boot!

Distant Horizons

On a distant shore, the stars conspire,
With giggles and hiccups, they never tire.
They throw a feast, lots of space snacks,
And chase the light on playful tracks.

With jellyfish swimming through the night,
They bounce around in sheer delight.
Here comes a rocket, all aglow,
With marshmallow engines, whoosh and go!

The sun peeks in, a cheeky grin,
'You thought I was gone? Let's begin!'
And all the stars give a playful push,
Creating a cosmic, shining hush.

So if you spot a flash on the run,
Don't just marvel, join the fun!
Bring your laughter, your joyful gaze,
And dance with the stars in a warm haze!

Dreams in Orbit

In circles bright, where dreams take flight,
The stars concoct a silly sight.
A doughnut-shaped moon joined the crew,
Rolling with laughter, oh what a view!

Each comet zipped with a playful cheer,
Shouting wishes, loud and clear.
Astro-bunnies hopped one by one,
Whisking through space just for fun.

Galaxies twinkled with playful tease,
While space dust swirled in a cosmic breeze.
The nebulas giggled with all their might,
Creating rainbows that danced through the night.

So plant your dreams, let them soar,
Cause every twinkle opens a door.
With laughter and joy as your guiding stars,
You'll paint the cosmos with zany sparks!

Ballet of the Night

In the dark, the stars do prance,
Doing the cha-cha in a cosmic dance.
Planets spin with silly flair,
Even comets stop to stare.

With twinkling eyes, they tease and laugh,
As if they're sharing a starry gaff.
The moon's a jester, wearing a grin,
While meteors slip on their own spin.

Galaxies swirl, a comical show,
Where black holes hide and giggles flow.
Each twinkle bursts like a joke unplanned,
Making the night feel rather grand.

So let us join this cosmic jest,
Where silliness reigns, and night's a fest.
Put on your shoes, take off your cares,
For the universe plays; who really dares?

Cosmic Harmony Unfolded

In the vastness, laughter roams,
Making space for funny poems.
Stars poke fun at what we do,
While aliens laugh, 'Is that really you?'

The sun bursts forth with a golden grin,
While planets giggle and join in.
Orbiting laughter around a joke,
Nebulae swirl in a colorful poke.

With asteroids rolling like bowling balls,
Echoes of giggles in cosmic halls.
Caution advised when taking a dive,
For black holes may suck up your vibe!

So let us tune to this playful hum,
While pulsars pulse and stardust drum.
Cosmic jokes, forever bold,
In the universe's comic fold.

Musing with the Moonlight

Under the glow of the cheeky moon,
I ponder thoughts that make me swoon.
She whispers jokes with a silvery flair,
While twinkling stars join in the air.

Backyard creatures are nodding along,
Even raccoons hum the happy song.
Fireflies flicker, 'Oh, what a night!'
As crickets join in with sheer delight.

Moonbeams stretch, like silly friends,
Wishing this humor never ends.
They giggle softly, causing a stir,
As shadows dance; oh, what a blur!

So let's revel in this lunar jest,
Where laughter conquers, and hearts are blessed.
With moonlight weaving a tale so bright,
We muse along with the cosmic light.

Melancholy of the Celestial Drift

In the void where lonely stars sigh,
A heartbroken comet asks, 'Why oh why?'
With a tail so long, it drags on the floor,
Wishing for laughs from a galactic galore.

Yet planets chuckle, offering cheer,
'Come join us, don't shed that tear!'
But black holes mumble, 'We can't relate,'
While supernovas start to celebrate.

Asteroids march, with grumpy faces,
Inspired by the moon's silly embraces.
Yet in this drift, small joys arise,
Beneath the frowns and clouded skies.

So while sadness flits, it won't last long,
In the echoes of starlight, life's a song.
Even when drifting through cosmic blues,
There's laughter awaiting in brilliant hues.

Galactic Echoes

In the night, a wink so bright,
It zoomed past, oh what a sight!
I chased its tail, what a race,
Tripped on my feet, fell on my face.

A comet yelled, 'Catch me if you can!'
But I just slipped, lost my plan.
With laughter loud, the stars did snicker,
As I spun around, getting quicker.

Big moments flash; then they're gone,
Like my snack stash after dawn.
A wink, a nod, twinkling glare,
While I wipe chocolate from my hair.

As planets danced, I took a bow,
A bit too hard, the ground said, "Wow!"
With every twirl and tumble bright,
I laughed with joy, it felt just right.

Radiance Beneath the Void

Stars look down with a knowing grin,
Did they spot my awful spin?
I reached for dreams and slipped on dreams,
Tumbled into cosmic schemes.

In the void, I tried to slide,
With a sparkle, oh I tried!
A nebula laughed, and so I fled,
'Stardust cowboy,' it lightly said.

Planets giggle, they think I'm nuts,
I just faceplanted, oh what a bust!
But moonbeams wink, "You'll land just fine,"
I swear, that's when the stars all shine.

Across the sky, with a goofy frown,
I'm the jester of this town!
Wherever I am, let laughter sail,
In this cosmic, carefree tale.

Echoes of a Faded Light

With a flicker light, a ghostly tease,
I thought I heard the stars all sneeze!
A twinkle brushed past with a tut,
"Don't trip on that space dust, you klutz!"

A cluster laughed, joined the jest,
While I tried to balance — it was a test!
Oh what folly, oh what charm,
As I swayed on stardust, with no alarm.

I shouted, "Hey! Is that a star?"
A comet replied, "You're way too far!"
With giggles echoing in the night,
I danced alone, feeling so light.

Thus, I wove through this cosmic riddle,
While the moon played music, what a fiddle!
In the realm of gleams, I'm a silly sprite,
Chasing echoes, in pure delight.

Transient Twinkles

A flash of light, oh where are you?
I tried to catch it, but who knew?
A meteor tickled my silly hair,
And sent me spinning through the air!

Galaxies giggle, their humor bright,
'Here comes the blunder, oh what a flight!'
I puffed and panted, the chase was grand,
But tripped on my shoelace, oh what a stand!

Stars dance round like they're at a ball,
While I tumble, trip, and do a down fall.
Yet every moment, packed with glee,
They shine for me, oh can't you see?

So here's to moments, loud and bright,
Where laughter sparkles through the night!
Stars may tease, but I can't complain,
In this cosmos, joy reigns again.

Threads of Light

In the sky, a spark so bright,
Whizzing past, what a sight!
Did you see that flashy glow?
No, that was just my toe!

Wishes fly, but wait, oh dear!
Tried to catch one, lost my beer.
Landing on the grass, what fun!
A little game, but I'm the pun.

Twinkling tails and goofy beams,
Dancing 'round like wild daydreams.
They say reach high, but I just fall,
Maybe next time, I'll give my all!

A comet zooms, it makes me laugh,
My friends are jealous, take a gaffe.
But in this night, let's not care,
We share the stars, and drink the air!

Heart's Nightfall

The moon grins wide, a funny chap,
While I trip over my own clap.
Do stars chuckle in the abyss?
Or are they just out for a bliss?

Whispers of love, but where's my shoe?
Made a wish, but I lost my crew.
A wink from Mars, with a bright flare,
I'll send a text, but who's aware?

My heart skips beats like a record spun,
Falling for laughter, just for fun.
Did I just see a shooting pie?
Or maybe that was a burger high?

So let's divide the night with glee,
And toast to stars, just you and me.
With giggles framed in moonlight bright,
Let's dance through this whimsical night!

Veils of Stardust

Draped in dust, the cosmos plays,
Twinkling jokes in starlit rays.
Did that star just wink at me?
Or was it just my latest spree?

From golden beams to cosmic bites,
The universe spins, igniting lights.
Falling laughter, a meteor's flight,
Ready to party, oh what a night!

With every wink, a secret shared,
My dreams go wild, so unprepared.
What's that noise? Oh, can't you tell?
It's just the stars's joke to quell.

So weave the night with giggles loud,
Under veils where dreams are proud.
We'll tie the laughs with ribbons bright,
As stardust sings, oh what a sight!

Skyward Whispers

Up above, the night sky jests,
A million jokes, it never rests.
The clouds are snickering all around,
As I trip over my own sound.

Wishes float like popcorn tight,
Popping dreams in sheer delight.
Did I just hear a comet's fool?
Or maybe that's just a goofy pool?

In this laughter, we find our place,
With galaxies in a silly race.
Stars zoom past, a crazy crew,
Making wishes, a dorky view.

So let's lift off to cosmic cheer,
Where smiles twinkle and hover near.
Together we'll dance, get quite absurd,
With skyward whispers, feel the word!

Flickering Fantasies

In the night sky they twinkle bright,
Whispering dreams that take flight.
With a wink and giggle, they dash past,
A cosmic joke, oh how they last!

Fishes in the air, oh what a scene,
Dancing like they're in a green cuisine.
Bouncing off clouds like silly balloons,
Painting the dark with cartoonish tunes!

A cat on a skateboard, upside down,
Waving wildly, wearing a crown.
Stars shake hands and share a laugh,
Cosmic clowns on a shining path!

While earthlings dream of touching their glow,
They're busy crafting a comedy show.
So catch a wish, though it's absurd,
And laugh with the cosmos, let joy be heard!

Cosmic Reflections

In the vastness, they gleam and slide,
Reflecting giggles from the other side.
A bounce in their glow, they mock the sun,
Making the moon blush, oh what fun!

Mirrors of laughter, twinkling bright,
Seeing our faces, what a delight!
A celestial game of peek-a-boo,
With every shimmer, they giggle too!

Comets spin like tops in a race,
Chasing their tails in a stellar space.
Noisy meteors, with a wink, they fly,
Leaving little trails of jokes in the sky!

As we gaze up, mouths agape,
Cosmic jesters in a playful shape.
Catching wishes with an awkward dance,
In this universe, we share a chance!

Illumined Journeys

Across the sky, they play and prance,
With trails of smiles, they love to dance.
On a magical ride, what a sight,
Where even the stars wear colors bright!

Riding comets, making a fuss,
Shooting through space on a cosmic bus.
They stop for snacks in a nebula's shop,
Chugging on stardust, never want to stop!

A party of lights, the universe sings,
Each little star is a quirky thing.
Carrying wishes on colorful wings,
Hitching a ride on the joy that springs!

With every flash, they break into cheer,
A constellation of jokes we hold dear.
So here's to the trips through night's endless sea,
Let's paint the sky with laughter, just you and me!

Nebulous Sighs

In fuzzy clouds where giggles reside,
Nebulas chuckle with playful pride.
Each sigh a shimmer, a wink, a tease,
As starlit giggles flutter like leaves.

Snickers and tinkles in splashes of hue,
Their bright little grins shine bold and true.
With whispers of mischief carried on air,
They play peek-a-boo without a care!

A soft cosmic chuckle fills the night,
As planets revolve in pure delight.
They snort with joy, oh what a sight,
The universe giggles, it's all so bright!

So when you wish upon their flight,
Remember the laughter hidden in light.
For in the silence of the starry sky,
Are ticklish echoes that flutter by!

Melodies Under the Milky Way

In pajamas, we dance on the lawn,
While stars giggle and tease with a yawn.
Crickets join in with a chirpy hum,
As moonlight spills laughter, oh what fun!

The Milky Way sparkles like spilled glitter,
We moonwalk and trip; our feet start to jitter.
Planets are winking; they know our delight,
With each silly twirl, we embrace the night.

Comets giggle as they whip by fast,
"Careful now, don't let that moment pass!"
Space chips in laughter, a cosmic delight,
Under the stars, we dance until light.

So, join the rhythm of the night's sweet song,
With celestial buddies, you can't go wrong.
Each twinkle's a chuckle, each sparkle a grin,
Let's sway with the cosmos, let the fun begin!

Ballet of Celestial Bodies

On a cosmic stage, the planets prance,
Stardust slippers in a whimsical dance.
Saturn spins lightly with a hula hoop,
While Mars does the cha-cha with an alien troupe.

Neptune twirls wildly, a ballerina's dream,
While comets go zooming on a light-speed beam.
The sun's like a DJ, spinning tracks for the night,
As meteors boogie, a dazzling sight.

Jupiter's got moves, oh so grand and bold,
Rings of gas swirling like fabric unrolled.
Winking at Earth, the stars cheer us on,
In this cosmic ballet that goes until dawn.

So wear your best sparkles and join in the fun,
Where laughter and stardust twirl in the sun.
As we dance with the planets, let your worries go,
In this whimsical ballet where laughter will flow!

Twinkling Tales of the Cosmos

Gather 'round friends for a story or two,
From the sparkly cosmos, where giggles ensue.
A puny little asteroid tried to impress,
With jokes so bad, he caused some distress.

Constellations chuckle at each silly joke,
As stars form a circle and share their bespoke.
A nebula whispers, "Did you hear that pun?"
Even black holes smirk, now that's quite the run!

Galaxies giggle with a light-hearted glee,
Lighting up the night with their winks full of spree.
Oh, what a circus on this cosmic stage,
Where each twinkling tale is a brand new page!

So let's toast to laughter, cosmic humor so bright,
In a universe buzzing, till we say goodnight.
With tales spun in stardust, we'll dance and we'll dream,
Under the laughter of a celestial beam!

Chasing Infinity

In bright sneakers, we race through the night,
Chasing the starlight with glittering flight.
The Milky Way laughs as we run down the lane,
With comets for company, we'll never feel pain.

"Hey, catch me if you can!" quips a nearby star,
As we leap and we bound, hoping to go far.
Galactic giggles echo in the dark,
With aliens cheering from the edge of a park.

The universe beckons, come join the parade,
With wormholes of wonder and cosmic cascade.
In this joyful chase, we'll find our way through,
With each twist and turn, discovering something new.

So lace up your shoes, let's take off, oh so spry,
In this funny race where laughter can fly.
Chasing infinity with a skip and a hop,
With the cosmos behind us, we'll never stop!

Beneath the Astral Canopy

Under the twinkly lights we dance,
A comet zooms by, what a chance!
We trip on wishes, spill our drinks,
And laugh at how the cosmos winks.

The moon's a pie, we want a slice,
Grabbing stars, oh isn't that nice!
But gravity pulls us back down,
While we giggle, wearing our crowns.

Aliens wave, they seem quite pleased,
We tell them jokes as we get teased.
They offer us green snacks to munch,
We munch, we chomp, it's quite the lunch!

So let's make wishes, loud and bright,
As we dance in the soft moonlight.
The universe chuckles, can you hear?
We'll be the stars in the sky, my dear!

Lullabies of the Night Sky

Hush now, the sky sings a tune,
With crickets strumming on a spoon.
The stars play hopscotch up there,
While we wiggle in cushioned chairs.

Dreams bounce around like bouncy balls,
As owls make their funny calls.
The night's a clown in the moon's bright beam,
Where even shadows giggle and scheme.

We lie on grass and make our vows,
To name each star, like odd-looking cows!
With each wish made, we burst out laughing,
As the universe joins in, crafting.

So close your eyes, let's fly away,
To the cosmic circus where we'll play.
With galaxies dancing, and meteors sliding,
This jolly night sky keeps providing!

Echoes of Starlit Dreams

Whispers of starlight tease our ears,
As we trip over dreams and cheers.
One bouncing star yelled out, 'Hey there!'
We laughed, forgetting our own despair.

Moonbeams juggled, and comets pranced,
While planets wobbled in a dance.
We chased the twinkles with silly shouts,
And slipped on cosmic giggles throughout.

Each twinkling note is a melody sweet,
As we dance barefoot on starry feet.
Shooting through the void, we share a joke,
With the universe laughing till it choked.

So close your eyes, let's tread the beams,
In the land where nothing's as it seems.
Falling through laughter, above silly streams,
We find the echoes of our dreams!

Cosmic Melodies in the Void

In the void, we hear a tune,
Made by dandelions in bloom.
Each puff sends planets swirling 'round,
As we giggle at the cosmic sound.

Galactic hiccups make us snort,
As supernovas play a sport.
We wear hats made of starlit dust,
As we prance, oh it's a must!

Laughter echoes through the night,
As galaxies hold a karaoke fight.
The asteroids join in, casting shadows,
As we laugh from our cosmic meadows.

So here we are, lost in delight,
Riding comets, holding on tight.
In this merry void, we plan our quest,
To find the universe's cheekiest jest!

Illuminated Yearnings

In the night sky, dreams take flight,
With a twinkle, they dance, oh what a sight!
Each wish a comet, racing past,
While I sit here, holding my breath, aghast.

Gravity just loves to play,
As I dream of worlds far away.
I shout my wishes with all my might,
And hope they don't crash in mid-flight.

A candy bar falls from my hand,
Like a meteor, it makes a stand.
Splattered chocolate, what a delight,
My midnight snack, now part of the night.

"Catch that one!" I yell at the moon,
As my dreams scoot off, they sing a tune.
But they're just too fast, gone in a flash,
Leaving me behind, a tumbler of trash.

Kindred in the Cosmos

With a wink and a nod, the stars align,
Telling jokes from beyond the divine.
They giggle as they tumble and sway,
Sharing secrets in the Milky Way.

I once saw a star trying to sneeze,
It sparkled and shimmered, oh what a tease!
An explosion of glitter, what a mess,
I laughed out loud, I must confess.

My buddy up there, with a big golden grin,
Trips on a cloud, and then comes the spin.
Down he goes, like a lopsided kite,
"Watch out below!" I yell with delight.

As meteors race in a brilliant show,
They must know the jokes that we don't know.
"Hey you!" I shout, "Don't leave me in the dust!"
But they just keep laughing, it's a galactic must!

A Dance of Light

The day fades out, the moon takes lead,
Stars light the floor, it's time to heed.
They twirl and spin in a cosmic jest,
Making the night feel like a fest.

I join their party, with feet on the ground,
While they twist and whirl all around.
"Hey, moon, save me a dance!" I plea,
But she's too busy, high and free.

The planets are waltzing, what a sight!
One crashes into another, oh, what a fright!
"Oops!" they laugh, with a twinkling shine,
"Let's do it again, it'll be just fine!"

And comets zoom in, with tails like gowns,
They shake and shimmer, they're wearing crowns.
I tap my feet, trying to keep pace,
While they giggle and swirl in a space embrace.

Celestial Apparitions

In a dream I saw colors all ablaze,
From ribbons of light, in cosmic lays.
Some silly ghost gave me a fright,
As he danced around in the pale moonlight.

"Boo!" he cried, and I stifled a laugh,
His ghoulish moves were quite the gaffe.
"Come join us here!" he beckoned with glee,
With a twinkle, he scattered light confetti.

Galaxies giggled at their friend's quirk,
As they spun around, what a bizarre perk!
"Who needs sleep in this cosmic ballet?"
They erupted in laughter—oh, what a day!

Stardust dripped like candy from above,
Decorating the night with cosmic love.
I shook my head, sipping space juice,
As the ghosts took a leap, oh, what a rouse!

Celestial Cascade

Up in the sky, oh what a flight,
With tacos and cheese, they dance at night.
Nebulae giggle, comets can't wait,
For space guacamole on a stellar plate.

Asteroids bounce like a cosmic ball,
While planets laugh, having a great sprawl.
Galactic donuts circle round in flair,
Who knew space could be this rare?

Aliens joke with their green little heads,
Telling tales of far-off bread spreads.
In this cascade, joy's the key,
As they bounce on the rings of a Jovian spree.

With each twinkle, an echo of cheer,
The universe chuckles, oh so near.
In a whirlwind of laughter, we glide and spin,
Creating memories, where do we begin?

Echoes from the Abyss

In the deep void, a laugh emerges,
Where shadows frolic and chaos surges.
A fish in a bowtie, swims with flair,
Echoes of giggles travel everywhere.

Squids with umbrellas float on by,
While jellyfish smile as they drift and sigh.
The abyss is a stage, a wild, weird show,
Where even the stars can't help but glow.

Bubbles like jokes, they rise and pop,
In the silence of space, they make hearts hop.
A cosmic ballet of odd little blunders,
Lost in the laughs, amid the wonders.

With a wink and a nudge, time takes a pause,
As laughter escapes from unearthly jaws.
From the depths of space, what a display,
Echoes of nonsense lead the way!

Celestial Romancing

Two stars are twirling, what a delight,
In a ball of gas, they shine so bright.
With glittery glances and cosmic designs,
They serenade the universe with silly lines.

Asteroids whisper sweet nothings, so grand,
While meteors moonwalk, hand in hand.
In the sky's grand theatre, love's on the stage,
Rewriting the rules, page by page.

Saturn's rings sway like a dance floor's beat,
As planets groove to an interstellar treat.
With every spin, romance bursts free,
Exploding like confetti, oh, what jubilee!

Together they wander, drift, and sway,
In this cosmic play, they find their way.
With each turn of fate, there's laughter to chase,
In the dance of the stars, we see their grace!

Cosmic Contemplations

In the vastness of space, what should we think?
With black holes and aliens that often wink.
Should we ponder the moons or watch comets race?
Or maybe just snack on celestial paste?

Planets debate their colors and sizes,
While stardust makes mischief in all its disguises.
The sun cracks jokes that tickle the night,
As the universe chuckles, oh, what a sight!

Galaxies gather to share their dreams,
While quasars giggle at space-time schemes.
With laughter like echoes that bounce through the void,
In this cosmic realm, no one's annoyed.

So let's sit back and enjoy the show,
With cosmic jesters putting on flow.
In this wild expanse, joy never fades,
It's a circus of stars, where laughter parades!

www.ingramcontent.com/pod-product-compliance
Lightning Source LLC
Chambersburg PA
CBHW072142200426
43209CB00051B/256